Are We There Yet

BRYAN BRUMLEY
My Name Is Nobody

GRAPH Publishing, L.L.C.

Copyright © 2024
All rights reserved.

No part of this book may be reproduced or transmitted in any form or by any means, electronic or mechanical, including photocopying, recording, or by any information storage and retrieval system, without permission in writing from the copyright owner.

Published by
GRAPH Publishing, L.L.C.
www.graphpublishing.com

Printed in the U.S.A.

About The Author

The author "My Name is Nobody," or Bryan Brumley who is a husband of twenty six years and a parent of two. He became a jack of all trades and master of none as he and his wife provided for their family and followed their nomadic traits. After an Apostle Paul experience that he describes in the book "Poetry in Motion", he felt a calling that the Lord would use his change and experiences, to make a better servant for the work of The Great Commission. His experience from his different professions like oilfield, chainsaw artist, machinist, carpenter and international transport driver; plus hobbies like woodworking and a lifelong passion for martial arts gave him a perspective that helps him to relate to so many, along with his own experiences growing up in a broken home as so many do these days. It all "really" is a book of its own. His relationship to Jesus the Christ helped him to be empathetic and to always try to see things from other people's perspective. His goal or mission is to use every possession, talent and experience blessed to him, to not only tell about Jesus and what he has and is still doing, but to also shine light on lucifer, lucifer's plans, and not only his beastly system, but those that would follow it also, whether it be on purpose or by accident, regardless whether it was out of laziness or simply a lack of knowledge and desire to know.

Are We There Yet

During my life, I have worked many years chasing oilfield money. Living in a small town in Texas, I was employed all of those years with a small company that worked seven days a week. The only days off came if we could not move the drilling rig due to weather, and it wasn't often that the weather beat out the dozers. Being a small town company, it refused to run a five man crew when five is what it took to do the job safely, working everyone seven days a week. Instead, we ran four men crews. This is the real oilfield I am talking about. With real roughnecks, not the puff-necks that are like steering wheel holders. I am talking spinning chain, cat heads, rotary table, U-15 draw works and duplex pumps. Everything bought from an auction, which meant everything was worn out already making every day a battle to keep it all running. Because of the workload, many of the employees were on drugs in order to keep up with the demand. This is why drug testing only really happened when someone was injured, to avoid claims. This is also why most of these businesses slowly go out of business when forced to start doing random drug tests. They run out of druggies that are willing to do the workload required. The motto became, " if you won't do it, we will find someone that will." Because of the quality of the workers, most of the time the team consisted of three people when it should have been a team of four, because druggies are always twisting off and being flaky. This would cause an already overworked hand to stay over for another shift. This happened often enough that most floor hands knew very well how to make a one man connection.

    I do not mention all of this to belittle a company for chasing the same money I was chasing. I did it for fourteen years and we each agreed to the job and the pay. It ended up being a good lesson of knowing one's own worth. I mention all of this because it took some specific people to be able to work in these conditions, hence the title of roughneck. Do not get me wrong, there were and still are those hard enough to do the workload without drugs, many were not. A lot of roughnecks had history in prison, since the oilfield did not care about their background, only that they did what they did and what they were told without question. Because of this, I became friends with many ex-prisoners and learned a bit about the prison system and life in it. It is also how a non drug user learned so much about drugs. In a way, it was like working in the middle of an experiment where I saw the results first hand. After about fourteen years in the old school oilfield, oh do I have stories!

 One of the things I noticed, was that the oilfield atmosphere was good for a lot of men that came out of prison. Not the expected work load, but the body that a drilling rig represents. The operation of the drilling rig gave everyone a common goal to work towards. Each crew had a driller that had "three" hands under him. The driller answered to the tool pusher and the tool pusher worked for his company that was drilling for another company. Therefore it taught a chain of command. When a rig is doing well, it's when everyone has learned to see themselves as a body part serving a function that benefits the whole body. Everyone learns first hand what happens when a body part isn't pulling their own weight, or everyone is gunning after everyone else's job. It all slowly falls apart. I was blessed enough to experience for four years as a driller, how smooth things can run with a crew that understands and cares about their part, that looks after one another but does not race after their job, respects the whole body and the chain of command. Each day at work with the crew was like watching poetry in motion. I also experienced (after being a tool pusher for several years), how a rig can fall apart when the pusher neglects his duties, and the rig hands get lost going after the jobs of others, instead of focusing on their job for the day.

 Something that I found interesting after so long of asking questions from former inmates, is the number given to a prisoner after given a psychological evaluation. This number is a three digit number given after completing the evaluation. This number plays a large role on whether a prisoner will be paroled or not. This number becomes the identity of the prisoner. The problem with the number is that it's formulated by a series of questions. These questions are about past and present decisions. Once the questions are asked, a calculation is done and a number is assigned. The higher the number, the more psychotic potential a person has and therefore should not be released into the public. Most "normal" scores are between forty four and one hundred and twenty, so a score that goes over six hundred would be considered in the psychotic category.

    The first problem with this number is that the questions focus a lot on past decisions. Very little of the overall score is derived from one's current state of mind, giving a very unfair and deliberate focus on past mistakes, and not enough deserving focus on current changes and growth. The system does not even make a real effort to correct the behavior that puts many in prison. Only locks them up in an environment that breeds despair and selfishness. Too many do not ask questions about how the prison system worked in Jesus's day. Notice in his parables, a man went to jail until his debt was paid? How does one pay a debt while in jail unless the jail worked them? Yet I am guessing that most are supposed to miraculously learn their lesson and know better? To learn to do better in this monkey see-monkey do world, one needs to be able to "see" what "better" looks like, and maybe even experience it. It is hard for a spoiled people to understand, but the truth is, many have never seen a good example to follow. Many have never known a safe place or a person to trust and believe in. Who does some of the blame fall on when a repeat offender keeps going back to a "corrections" facility?

    The second problem is also within the questions. Not only are there an unfair number of questions about past mistakes, but many of those questions are the same question, just asked in a different way. So one gets penalized for the same past mistakes multiple times. All rolling into a three digit score that they are identifying a person by. I am not saying that this number given to prisoners is the mark of the beast, but this number does in a way, become the number of a man, if one is a prisoner. As does a phone number, social security number and for many, even a credit score number. Many of which are already rapidly becoming necessary to be able to function in society. They are needed in order to buy, sell, or trade in the system. There are already stores that one cannot enter to buy food and supplies if a person cannot show them their mark. Sam's Club is one of them.

Now imagine a socialistic society that judged every person by a psychological evaluation. I wouldn't think it would be very hard to imagine a single person or entity to "mandate" something like that these days. It would become the number that identifies every person's worth, or "goodness", "the number of a man."

Revelation 13:16-18

16) And he causeth all, both small and great, rich and poor, free and bond, to receive a mark in their right hand, or in their foreheads:
17) And that no man might buy or sell, save he that had the mark, or the name of the beast, or the number of his name.
18) Here is wisdom. Let him that hath understanding count the number of the beast: for it is the number of a man; and his number is six hundred three score and six.

Again, I am not saying that the number is the same number given to a man in prison, but I am not going to rule out the possibility that a government wouldn't "mandate" a "psychological evaluation" on every citizen, then place them in society based or judged on their number or "goodness", with your three digit credit score judging ones worth and being identified by one's social security number. It would be very easy for a socialistic government to "mandate" such a thing under penalty of not being able to buy or sell. How many "mandates" did Joe Biden do in the first six months of his monarchy? Imagine how bipolar that made Americans look to other countries. It definitely did not make America look "United" or of one accord. It is very important for us all to keep an eye out for the signs of the mark of the beast. We have to always ask ourselves, are things ripe for something like this to happen? Are things getting to where a single person or entity can "mandate" such a thing on a world wide scale? Are things to the point to where a single person or entity, can keep you from buying or selling if you did not follow their command, or carry in your wallet what they told you to carry?

    The answer is yes. Things are rapidly becoming possible for a single person to "mandate" a mark under penalty of not being able to buy or sell. The sad part is seeing how sinful mandates make many react. Which is one of lucifers's goals, making the innocent turn on each other. It is like a sport to him. We saw with the "Covid mandates" in 2021, how it made people react to one another. Just like with vaccines, we know that there will be those that take the beasts "mandated" mark and those that won't. From experience, we all know that there will be people envious and regretful after they take the mark, to the point of turning on friends and family.

Matthew 10:21-22

21)   "And the brother shall deliver up the brother to death, and the father the child: and the children shall rise up against their parents, and cause them to be put to death.
22)   And ye shall be hated of all men for my name's sake; but he that endureth to the end shall be saved."

    Do we see in our own times and society where it looks like families will turn on their own families? Has a beastly system slowly destroyed families and their values learned from God? Does a beastly system make it hard for families to live and be like Jesus says to? Instead of living for the profit of all, does this beastly system remove the things of God to better encourage the obsession with self and selfish things. And again, does this beastly system have the power yet, to "mandate" a mark on all mankind, regardless of what the mark is?

"If it will go an inch, it will go a mile." This is a saying that my toolpusher would always tell me while I was a driller on a drilling rig. Thanks to his perspective on the job, I walked away from a fourteen year oilfield career being able to say I never got stuck. Depending on how stuck a rig gets, it could cost a company a lot of money to get unstuck. Sometimes even having to cement and start new in another spot. Every time I would call to let him know we were pulling tight and I called the derrick man down, he would ask me if it was moving. A lot of lazy drillers get tired and give up, especially when we only gain an inch at a time and have thousands of feet to go. When I would tell him it is moving an inch at a time, he would always say, "if it will go an inch, it will go a mile." So I would continue to work it, trying to get it through before he got there. It sometimes took hours, but it always came out. You know the pusher, Bruce Willis played in the movie Armageddon? This pusher would have been that guy, I learned a lot from him. I've also learned that lucifer also uses this philosophy. He knows that he can make big changes over a very long period of time by moving an inch at a time. And just like us moving mountains with equipment, it sometimes takes so long that it goes unnoticed to the majority, especially if the majority is moving too fast chasing fruitless things.

    This also brings to mind another of lucifer's tactics to usher in his beastly system and mark. In order to gain trust when dealing with animals, many trainers will tell you that touch is important. The more you can get a horse or any animal used to a slight touch, the better, you then slowly increase the amount and pressure over time until the animal is comfortable with you and does not question you anymore. These two tactics combined is what lucifer has been doing for thousands of years, getting the world used to his touch so he can brand his mark on everyone he owns. "If it will go an inch, it will go a mile." And unnoticed if done slowly over hundreds or thousands of years, it brings a new look to the phrase, "faster, faster, we need a new master." Lucifer wants to be the new "master" and he is fooling us all to move faster and faster just to survive, so we do not see him moving.

I also learned about the logic of much of this in my life's pursuit of martial arts. We learn certain things from martial arts and one of those things is about vision. Even though I learned this years before, there is a very well educated man that teaches on these things. His name is "John La Tourrette". Since I call no man master, I will say that he has multiple black belts in multiple arts as well as a degree in sports psychology and has experience training police and military. As I started learning about vision and how it all works, I started testing it with my son. You see, perefrial vision picks up motion, fobial vision does not. As we played the game of trying to sneak up on each other, we learned the truth of these facts. We both got to the point where we would have to belly crawl, because we kept expecting each other. Our awareness and perefrial got better to the point that whoever was sneaking, was having to move like a snail or the perefrial of the other would pick up the movement. Too be honest, my cracking ankles gave me away a lot. I had to get better and move slower because my son rearranged his room to a defensive arrangement, lol. He actually got to the point in his awareness, that he knew when I entered his room because he felt my body shift the air in the room. Does one know how slow one has to move to not shift still air? The point being, that lucifer knows these things as well and knows, "if it will go an inch; it will go a mile". He is sneaking up on everyone while we all are too busy going faster and faster, chasing selfish things. Because of this, we do not feel the shift as lucifer is re-steering all of humanity, until we do not notice his touch anymore and has all of his numbered cattle branded with a mark.

I find it interesting that the mark of the beast is a number. The number given in revelation is 666 and is "his" number, meaning the Beast or the Antichrist. It is the number of his name. The mark is a number but not specific to his number alone as the mark. Before I explain this part, I have a question that needs consideration. If I knew that 3 enemies were planning to beat you up and enslave you, and I only warned you about 1 of them, would that make me your brother? Would that make me a friend? Now let's look at Revelation 13:17 closely and see what seeds by the wayside have been plucked up by the birds.

Revelation 13:17

17)   And that no man might buy or sell, save he that had **the mark, or** the name of the beast, **or** the number of his name.

Notice there is an "or" after "the mark". What does "or" mean? It means there is another, which is "the name of the beast". Then there is a second "or", again, meaning there is another which is "the number of the beast". So there are three elements to the same mark that the Antichrist uses to mark his slaves as cattle. "Save those that had",

> 1) The mark, which is the number of a man.
>   Or
> 2) The name of the beast.
>   Or
> 3) The number of his name

The number 666 is not the only thing that constitutes the mark of the beast, as is seen simply in John's own words. So if we take the number of a man, we have taken "the mark". If we take the name of the beast, we have taken "the mark". If we take the number 666 which is the beast's number, we have taken "the mark". I find it interesting because I think back to 2 Samuel chapter 24.

2 Samuel 24:1;10-15;17

1)   And again the anger of the lord was kindled against Israel, and he moved David against them to say, go, number Israel and Judah.

10)   And David's heart smote him after that he had numbered the people. And David said unto the Lord, I have sinned greatly in that I have done; and now, I beseech thee, O

Lord, take away the iniquity of thy servant; for I have done very foolishly.

11) For when David was up in the morning, the word of the Lord came unto the prophet Gad, David's seer, saying,

12) Go and say unto David, thus sanity the Lord, I offer thee three things; choose thee one of them, that I may do it unto thee.

13) So Gad came to David, and told him, and said unto him, shall seven years of famine come unto thee in thy land? Or wilt thou flee three months before thine enemies, while they pursue thee? Or that there be three days pestilence in thy land? Now advise, and see what answer I shall return to him that sent me.

14) And David said unto Gad, I am in a great strait; let us fall now into the hand of the Lord; for his mercies are great: and let me not fall into the hand of man.

15) So the Lord sent a pestilence upon Israel from the morning even to the time appointed: and there died of the people from Dan even to Beersheba seventy thousand men.

17) And David spake unto the Lord when he saw the angel that smote the people, and said, Lo, I have sinned, and I have done wickedly; but the sheep, What have they done? Let thine hand, I pray thee, be against me, and against my Father's house.

While there is a lot to learn from these verses, like a people that claims to be of God is held to a different standard than the rest of the world. Or like when we choose to be a Godly people and accept the protection and benefits yet ignore and mock his rules and commands, ignorance does not excuse us from his punishments, which include and are not limited to, plagues of pandemics, fields and lakes drying up and even being made slaves by another country. History is a non stop cycle of cultures being taken captive by other cultures. Cultures even do the same within themselves. These things come about when God removes his protection, and he only does this when either the people as a whole or its leaders fall away from God's ways and values. The great sin that David did in this story is numbering the people. Note that we are given the count of people repeatedly throughout the Bible, so it is not counting people to keep up with supplies that was the sin, he numbered them. Many might ask why this was considered a sin and was met with such a harsh punishment. It is because when we start numbering people like cattle, we start losing our love for humanity more rapidly. We no longer see humans as human beings anymore but a number like cattle. Those that were meant to serve, start seeing people as a burden to take care of and profit from, instead of the people they agreed to serve and help take care of. It starts the corporate mentality that wants everyone to be the same and easily controlled. Only caring about profits, the numbers. Unfortunately, technology will probably be the tool used by the Antichrist, and corporations will hold the leashes as it enslaves everyone. Again, God tells us not to do something and it shows lucifer and his ways, because lucifer cannot help but to force God's people to do what displeases God. Hence why the mark of the beast is either his name or a number of a man whether it is his or ours.

    Now think on the mark of the beast and on the fact that it is a number and said to be the number of a man. Think back to the Holocaust and how the Jews were numbered like cattle. Think back to any socialistic society and recall that its people are always "numbered". So many say that they would never take a mark, yet lucifer is preparing the world to take it without question if possible. His method, since he has had thousands of years, is almost exactly like breaking an animal or befriending a stray. It all starts with controlling and offering what they need most, food, water and shelter. Then it is getting them used to seeing and hearing us, getting them used to our presence. Next comes touch. We start with small touches until the animal lets us pet it. Next thing we know, we are petting then holding or riding the animal that didn't trust us at first. So many look at things like phone numbers, social security numbers and such, and think mark of the beast. I see all of these numbers as small touches by a beastly system, trying to get humanity used to the beast's touch. All so when this system rolls out the real mark, everyone is so used to being numbered and taking marks, nobody will recognize it for what it is. All because people that forgot about God, only vote in snakes that appeal to our selfishness, who slowly push God and his protection away from us. We now have the corrupt and blind leading the selfish and blind. We already have so many numbers in order to buy, sell or trade, will we really notice the "mandated" mark when the main Antichrist takes the stage for their part?

Now I say the main Antichrist because John tells us plainly that there are already antichrists in the world, in his own time. He goes on to tell us exactly what an antichrist is.

1 John 2:18-19;22-23

18) Little children, it is the last time: and as ye have heard the Antichrist shall come, even now are there many antichrists: whereby we know that it is the last time.

19) They went out from us, but they were not of us: for if they had been of us, they would no doubt have continued with us: but they went out, that they might be made manifest that they were not all of us.

22) Who is a liar but he that denieth that Jesus is the Christ? He is Antichrist, that denieth the Father and the Son.

23) Whosoever denieth the Son, the same hath not the Father: [but] He that acknowledgeth the Son hath the Father also.

John makes it clear that individuals can be called antichrists and they are identified by their refusal to see Jesus as the Son of God the Father. There are even those that do believe but still hide behind holy things to gain power and influence. For these we are told to look at the fruits of others because snakes hide easily behind words. Verse 19 warns that this Antichrist system of thought started out within them. But these systems left them and started their own. This new system starts out by first twisting Jesus's words then ignoring his commands, only to think to change times and laws of God the Father. The scripture that this system that separated itself from

God's chosen people is found in Matthew. This scripture is Jesus telling Peter what exactly his church will be built on, the rock and foundation of it.

Matthew 16:13-18

13) When Jesus came into the costs of Caesarea Philippi, he asked his disciples, saying, "whom do men say that I the son of man am?"
14) And they said, some say that thou art John the Baptist: some, Elias; and others, Jeremias, or one of the prophets.
15) He saith unto them, "but whom say ye that I am?"
16) And Simon Peter answered and said, <u>thou art the Christ, the Son of the living God.</u>
17) And Jesus answered and said unto him, "blessed art thou, Simon Barjona: for flesh and blood hath not revealed it unto thee, but my Father which is in heaven.
18) And I say also unto thee, that thou art Peter, and upon <u>this</u> rock I will build my church; and the gates of hell shall not prevail against it.

Because our selfishness will have us twist certain scriptures to justify our sin, this system of thought that separated itself because it envied the control and power that the Scribes and Pharisees had over their people, twisted Jesus's words. This whole conversation between Jesus and the Apostles is about who Jesus is because that is the question Jesus asked. After Simon tells Jesus who everyone else says that he is, Jesus asks Simon specifically who he thought Jesus was. Simon simply answers that he believed Jesus was the Christ, the Son of the living God. Jesus changed Simon's name to Peter, then tells him that he answered correctly and that God revealed this truth to him, not man, and that this fact is the rock his church will be built on. The foundation that hell will not prevail against is that Jesus **is** the Christ, the Son of the living God. The lusts and envy of this new system twists Jesus's words, trying to say that because Peter means rock, that Peter was the foundation his church should be built on. Even though Jesus does not say upon you

Peter I will build my church. Again, lucifer's system of thought is given just enough room to assume that Peter's name change meant they could change Jesus's words. Just my opinion, but the Bible does a good job of teaching us how imperfect we all are, and that Jesus was the only perfect example. Stands to reason that his church would be built on him, not a sinful man. Jesus did say that he made it so simple that a child can comprehend it. Let us not complicate his simplicity with our selfish desires.

    With all of that aside, it is clear that the rock and foundation of Christ's church, which will be called a house of prayer, is the fact that he is the Christ, which means Messiah, and the Son of the living God, who Jesus himself shows us we are to see as our Heavenly Father. Making all who deny this fact an Antichrist, and the main Antichrist of the end will push a system that tricks and teaches to ignore scriptures and commands straight from Jesus. The other system of thought that separated from the apostles was those that believe in God, but not as the father. They did not believe or except Jesus as the Christ, as the messiah. They do not even believe Jesus to be the son of God. This system of thought belongs to many like the Muslim belief. Because this system denies that Jesus is the Christ and the son of God, as well as God as the Father, it makes them an antichrist system of thought. Their teachings even teach them to spread by doing and saying whatever it takes to infiltrate everywhere. All to water down and eventually try to exterminate the beliefs of Christ followers. The Antichrist will then use these systems of thought after they become global, to force his mark which will be one of 3 things, your number which will be considered the number of a man, the beast's name or the number which is 666 and is the number of the beast. Ever so slowly until the bridle and saddle are on. The forceful part comes as time runs out and too many people start waking up. I also have to mention the dangers involved in straying from the King James Version. Many seek easier and easier translations, mostly due to many not understanding that it is the Holy Ghost that unlocks our understanding at the right times when we are ready, which is why we can't just read it once and know everything. It is meant to be a lifetime read. I explain this in detail in the book "Poetry In Motion". We are given a warning in Revelation about those that would change the scriptures, especially the prophecies in Revelation themselves.

Revelation 22:18-19

18) For i testify unto every man that hearth the words of the prophecy of this book, if any man shall add unto these things, God shall add unto him the plagues that are written in this book:
19) And if any man shall take away from the words of the book of this prophesy, God shall take away his part out of the book of life, and out of the holy city, and from the things which are written in this book.

Now look at **Revelation 13:17** in the niv (new international version). Compare this verse to the King James Version.

17) so that they could not buy or sell unless they had the mark, which is the name of the beast or the number of his name.

    Notice how someone influenced by lucifer's system of thought ignores the warning John gives by removing the first "or"? Not only do they remove a word meant to let us know the multiple different marks, they then add words to hide the fact that there ever was multiple aspects to the same mark, setting things up for a beastly system to number masses without question because things have been added and taken away over time. Now this goes back to my earlier question, if I knew there were three different aspects to a mark and I was doomed if I took any one of the three, does that make me an enemy or friend if I purposely hid knowledge of one of these marks? Unfortunately there is more than one system that left the apostles to chase after power and control. One in particular likes to change or flat out ignore many scriptures.
    One of the many scriptures of this system that chose not to continue with the chosen ignores, just happens to be a

command from Jesus himself.

Matthew 23:9
9) "And call no man your father upon the earth: for one is your Father, which is in heaven."

This was not a suggestion or friendly request from Jesus. It was a command that he gave for a reason. As I mention in the book Poetry in Motion, commands telling us not to do something, always draws out lucifer and his, and the Bible is clear on ignoring commands no matter how small, and the last I checked, we are all still on Earth. And it isn't small in God's eyes if it misleads millions of his children.

1 John 2:4
4) He that saith, I know him, and keepeth not his commandments, is a liar, and the truth is not in him.

We can actually see as one of these systems of thought moves further from God's chosen, they continue to twist meanings and ignore commands chasing after the control the Pharisees had over their people. Harboring a desire to control salvation and forgiveness, making people believe forgiveness comes from them and has to be paid for by additional verbal or monetary sacrifices, like Jesus' sacrifice wasn't enough. Continually compromising their faith until a system is formed for the Antichrist to step into and implant the mark on a world mass that has been slowly bridled over time.

While there will be those that refuse to see the importance of this, as well as those that will continue to hide the three aspects of the mark that can doom us, I refuse to be shackled from behind because I choose to have tunnel vision. I do not believe our adversary to be dim witted. He had far longer than us as individuals to figure out how to twist things. So I continue to look for the signs of any mark that might be "mandated" in order for me to be able to live. Any mark that would cause families to turn against families. The small touches, trying to get us used to the bridle that everyone knows is coming. I try not to forget that the very mark is "mandated" by an individual or entity that has global power to do all of these things on a global scale. That this very person or entity makes war with God's people, which are those that believe in and follow Jesus's commands no matter how small, or even if we think he wasn't serious. When did Jesus ever joke about our salvation or the way to obtain it? I often ask myself if these things are possible now, or are they already happening?

If there was ever a time to remember the actual events of God's people in the wilderness, it is now.

Numbers 21:4-9

4) And they journeyed from Mount Hor by the way of the Red Sea, to compass the land of Edom: and the soul of the people was much discouraged because of the way.
5) And the people spake against God, and against Moses, wherefore have ye brought us up out of Egypt to die in the wilderness? For there is no bread, neither is there any water; and our soul loatheth this light bread.
6) And the Lord sent fiery serpents among the people, and they bit the people; and much people of Israel died.
7) Therefore the people came to Moses, and said, we have sinned, for we have spoken against the Lord, and against thee; pray unto the Lord, that he take away the serpents from us. And Moses prayed for the people.
8) And the Lord said unto Moses, make thee a fiery serpent, and set it upon a pole: and it shall come to past, that every one that is bitten, when he looketh upon it shall live.
9) And Moses made a serpent of brass, and put it upon a pole, and it came to pass, that if a serpent had bitten any man, when he beheld the serpent of brass, he lived.

The people became ungrateful and began complaining too much against God and Moses. Many chose not to recognize God at all by worshipping other things. This whole scenario is a cycle that repeats within God's chosen people. This may be a story from a long time ago, yet we see this same cycle laying out before us. We started out on Godly values. Many like to argue and say that we and others in the past did not start out on Godly morals and values. I would have to ask, do most cultures build on top of values that promote lying, stealing, murdering and disrespect to all? Or do most sociaties have a foundation that promotes honesty, prosperty and safety? These last are the values of God whether we accept it or not, and is what most societies are modeled after. Then the snakes start the cycle as they exploit our selfishness, which brings us once again to what we see today. As we prospered due to striving for godly values, we became comfortable and lazy. Eventually forgetting who our blessings come from. We let so much slip over time saying, "oh it's ok, it won't hurt anything", that we no longer breed enough people with godly values. The result is an infestation of snakes, corrupt from the inside out with their venomous logic and system of thought. Pushing God away until snakes are all that run things, turning a godly nation into one that resembles Sodom and Gomorrah, and we can read how that turned out. Many that disagree with this forget to realize that it is as simple as looking at workers. Workers with no godly morals and values have to be watched most of the time. I've seen bosses hide to spy on lazy workers. Those that truly believe and follow God do not have to be watched. Simply because they most times are doing the best they can all of the time for God, not merely their boss. They know God is always watching. Just like two people in different places that think they are all alone. One without godly morals and values might convince themselves to do something they would not normally do, all because they believe there is no eyes or law to catch or punish them. A true follower of Jesus would not because again, they know and believe that they are always being watched and judged by their actions. Kinda the story of Cain and Abel. One put his all into his gift to God while the other had half intent. Because of this, God chose Abel's gift over Cain's. And as always, the one that does things with half intent, gets jealous and harms those that God picks. These same types of people are still around today.

    These sinful followers of lucifer's system of thought have no vision of their own. This is why they enslave God's people in corrupt systems. Because they know that God blesses his people. They use twisted logic to enslave the people of God after they themselves have fallen asleep, then compromised their faith to the point that evil is able to rape the benefits of God's people. All so they can twist a world that makes evil feel better about being sick and twisted, until the world celebrates factory defects caused by our selfish disobedience, instead of trying to fix the assembly line. We then paint rainbows around our factory defects and try to make defects the new normal. Then promote murder to further rob people of the chance to choose salvation over selfishness. I know there will be so many that see this analogy as harsh. Unfortunately, there is no magic sentence that will make every person get it and understand. This is my best attempt. Defects happen in every production line, even the living one. And just like in all others, they happen for many various reasons. We do not belittle each other when we receive a defect notice. Just like with our vehicles, it mostly never effects how it runs. We get it fixed if we can, if we can't, we operate around it without letting it dominate us. What we do not do, is celebrate the defect to the point that we change the assembly line to produce only defects.

Nothing new under the sun. A cycle of God blessing those that remember and recognize him. When our complacency makes us too selfish and lazy, he has to send something to remind us that he is the creator and we are the created. In this story, God sent a plague of snakes and many people died, until they remembered who they were complaining about. God then made Moses put a brass serpent on a pole so that all who looked on it and believed, after being bitten, would live. Many might ask how this helps us today. The story passes down as a foreshadowing to teach us,

1) That God did not remove the plague, showing that we all are always subject to the snake's bite.
2) That the only cure for that old snake's venom, is to look back to the fiery serpent on the pole. Which for us today, the fiery pole is to look to Jesus and what he did for all on the cross. Jesus's own words in John shows us that the story in numbers is

meant to be a foreshadowing of what Jesus was to do and be for all of humanity.

John 3:14-15

14) "And as Moses lifted up the serpent in the wilderness, even so must the sun of man be lifted up:
15) That whosoever believeth in him should not perish, but have eternal life".

So many of us know the next verse by heart, John 3:16. So well that we often overlook the previous two verses, and what they reference to and how it points to how we can heal ourselves from that selfish venom, individually and as a nation. By turning our eyes back to Jesus and the cross he was raised on. Are we as a nation and as individuals being bit by that old serpent? Is his selfish venom spreading through our nation, causing our "public servants" to act like hungry, hungry hippos every time money, titles, and influence are discussed? Is the hen house becoming overrun by snakes that only care about personal interests, and are too cowardly to refuse being bought and paid off? Is his selfish venom creating a place where a single person or entity can "mandate" any mark without question and logic? We will know them by their fruit, which means actions, not words.

The answer to those questions is yes. I know that we like to blame our situations on someone other than ourselves. The truth of the matter is that we have nobody to blame but ourselves. America runs on a system of votes. Which means if nothing but corrupt individuals are running our country and changing our laws to allow them to fester, the people that voted them in have become corrupt, simple as that. Even if one only voted to get the free stuff. That means one voted from a heart of selfishness and therefore is corrupted, not thinking of the whole body or for the profit of all. In a voting system, the only way for the house to be full of snakes is if the country is full of snakes. And using John's definition of an antichrist, the only way for the main antichrist to rule, is for the majority to be turned into antichrists, which means a majority that does not believe Jesus is the Messiah and the son of God the Father, and the masses do not have to see this coming for it to happen. All because we allowed God and his protection to be removed because we believe the lies of serpents that promise empty dreams, instead of slowing down enough to search out the fruits of their labor and spirit.

    Can we fix it, and if so, how? Again, these answers and lessons are in the stories left to us. The story in numbers shows us the problem that cycles, as well as what to do to reverse the infestation of snakes. We turn our eyes back to Jesus, who turns our eyes back to the Father. Jesus is the way, he gives us the perfect examples to follow which injects God's values and system of thought back into a society that willingly removed them, and therefore removing his favor and protection. We should all know what happens to a culture after his favor and protection is removed. Their enemies move in to rape and pillage. Favor is something that God gives and takes away. Every historical biblical character we look up to, had God's favor. Which meant that at some point in their lives, they caught God's eye or attention. They usually have the heart of God, not afraid to stand up for him or the innocent. For example, David had God's favor. Daniel had God's favor. Sampson had God's favor, and just like in the story of Sampson, he lost it then had to learn to humble himself and admit and turn from the wickedness that lost him God's favor. What happened next in that story? God gave back a bit of the favor that gave Sampson his reputation. Just long enough to do another act for God's will.

    Here is a good example of not only how gaining favor can look, but also how druggies in the oilfield twist off leaving a crew in a bind. I had just started drilling and was on my first week. I had a derrick hand that was on drugs and two floor hands that hardly spoke English and was new to rig work, which meant they knew next to nothing. The derrick hand's duty is to look after the pumps and mud system while drilling and work up in the derrick when tripping pipe. I showed up one night as I drilled the graveyard shift, short handed because my derrick hand twisted off after payday, Leaving me with just the two new hands. Nobody from the previous tour wanted to stay over so we started the night short handed since we were drilling real slow. Back then slow drilling meant we might make one connection all night, so just keep everything running till daylight gets there, famous last words.

 One hour into the shift I hear the rotary table speed up. I go out to check the pump pressure and I have lost about one hundred and fifty pounds of pressure. I kick everything out and pick up on the drill pipe to see that I lost half of my string weight and another two hundred pounds of pump pressure, telling me we just twisted off. Meaning somewhere down the hole, the drill pipe twisted in half. I call my pusher and he tells me to start out of the hole. I tell him that my derrick hand twisted off on me so I have nobody to work the derrick board. He tells me to do the best I can because he is at a biker rally. So I put on the derrick belt, make preparations to trip out of the hole and start to work.

 It was slow going because I had to teach two hands that barely spoke English how to break connections and push the pipe back as I set it on the floor, all so I could then climb the derrick, unlatch the pipe, pull it back into the derrick then tie it off. Then climb down to do it again until we reach where it twisted at. Twenty seven stands later, the collar, which is the really thick pipe at the bottom of the string, was hanging twisted off with the other collars and drill bit still at the bottom of the hole. Daylight just started shining as the daylight crew showed up. I chained the brake handle down wearing a sweaty derrick belt, I looked back to see the daylight driller and his derrick hand looking at me smiling. The old driller looks at me then looks up and asks, "where is your derrick hand"? I told him he twisted off and is now fired. The daylight derrick hand looked at my two floor hands, took his hat off, put it over his heart and said, "I wouldn't have done it".

 After I dropped off the hands, I went to the office to look for a new derrick hand. I went into the owner's office and the pushing superintendent was talking with him. The old pusher smiled at me and asked why I didn't call him, he was over at his rig. I didn't want to get my pusher in trouble so I simply told him I had work to do so I got to it. He just grinned and nodded. After a few months he asked me to come over to his rig to run his daylight crew. I told him I would if I could bring my crew. By this time I had formed the crew that I drilled with for four years. I told him that he wants me because of my performance, I only get that performance because of my crew. He just grinned at me again and nodded. Me and that crew ran daylights on his rig for four years before I moved up to pusher myself. Because of my actions, I caught his attention and gained his favor. All because he saw someone that had a heart like his. Someone that would get the job done like he would have. We catch God's eye the same way. Except God looks for those that turns away from evil. Those with self control, which is what a lot of it boils down to. In the seven letters to the churches in Revelation 2:6, we learn that Jesus actually hates those with no self control. Which stands to reason since the commandments are all about self control. We steal because of lack of self control. We commit adultery, disrespect God and our parents all because of lack of self control. We lie and cheat our brothers because we lack the self control to choose good over selfishness. We get involved in sinful relationships because our lack of self control lets a little more slide each generation saying, "it's ok, it won't hurt anything", until we have a majority doing the deeds of Sodom and Gomorrah. Even now we have women and young girls that can't keep their legs closed. We have men and young boys that are too eager to dip their dipstick, all because of no self control. Because of this lack of self control, we twist logic to justify murdering innocence instead of slowing back down to learn self control. Bullies even belittle those that try to hang onto their virginity all to cover their own lack of self control. Many twist logic so they never see how much more self control and willpower it takes to tell our bodies no. We ask why America is going down hill yet refuse to see the signs and signals that America overall, has lost its self control and has lost God's favor because of it.

    This brings us to why fasting and prayer is so important. Why there are so many things to fast from as well as different lengths of fasts. There are different lengths of fasting which include one day, three days, seven days, twelve days, fourty days and even perpetual fasts. Even though too many only teach or talk about fasting from food, we can fast from anything that our body desires and that we can tell it no. This is how we show Jesus, who hates those with no self control, that we are serious about the prayer and purpose of our fast. This also exercises our self control muscles, making us better and better at controlling ourselves. Notice in 1 Corinthians 7:5, that we are told not to withhold from our spouses, meaning our affections, except for reasons of prayer and/or fasting. We do not withhold out of punishment, because the scriptures are clear that this allows satan to tempt us, and we can't complain much for the consequences for ignoring scriptures. We were meant to use this as a fasting and prayer tool that helps us gain favor as we build our self control over our bodily desires. The priests in the Old Testament even asked if the men have withheld from touching a woman. They had to make sure before giving the blessings. The fasting gave the soldiers favor on the battlefield due to their show of self control. There is power in fasting and prayer and lucifer knows these things, which is why he works hard to keep the teeth pulled out of God's people. He does this by watering down systems and plucking up seeds by the wayside. All so we forget what we are told to remember or never learn the lessons and examples left to us in the scriptures. Lessons and exercises meant to help us increase in the very thing Jesus says he hates that we do not have, self control. It is self control that helps us to "go and sin no more" like Jesus commands the women he saved from being stoned. He did not say try not to get caught again. He did not even tell her to try harder. He told her to "go and sin no more". Which means we are to strive for that daily. Learning from the lessons given on fasting and prayer. To build our self control so we can get better one day at a time controlling our selfish desires. So that the Holy Ghost can touch the world through us more than lucifer and his. Helping to turn all bad things to good.

So let us be diligent in showing our brothers and sisters what and who we need to put our eyes back on. Let us do it with love and kindness. Understanding that we all get bit from time to time. We all suffer from the symptoms of selfishness from time to time because they are numerous and well hidden. When we remember our own struggles, it helps us better understand each other and how to help. Jesus gave us all the information we need to have our lamps full so we are burning bright when he returns. We only need to endure to the end, trying to keep our eyes on him, because in an ever changing world, he is the only thing that stays the same. We protect each other by remembering the tricks of that old serpent, what he is after and what he needs to make it all happen. For those that say that lucifer does not need anything, he needs us. He needs us to let him get away with it all. There are also those that say there is no hope and that we cannot change things. I would remind them that there are those that not only believe that change is possible, but try to rob souls of a chance to accept Jesus by attempting to speed things up. Change is possible or we would not be told that if his people would humble themselves and turn from wickedness, he would heal their nation.

2 Chronicles 7:14

14) If my people, which are called by my name, shall humble themselves, and pray, and seek my face, and turn from their wicked ways; then will I hear from heaven, and will forgive their sins, and will heal their land.

May the Lord grant us the empathy to have patience and understanding, remembering our own struggles. May he grant us wisdom to watch out for the adversary and to remember to keep our eyes on who sacrificed themselves for us. May he grant us courage and strength to endure to the end, asking ourselves often, Are we there yet? Are we ready to be there?

In the name of Jesus the Christ, Amen.

       Love Lots And Pray Often
       One Day At A Time
       My Name Is Nobody

www.ingramcontent.com/pod-product-compliance
Lightning Source LLC
LaVergne TN
LVHW051227070526
838200LV00057B/4635